Leaving My Homeland

A Refugee's Journey from El Salvador

El Salvador

Linda Barghoorn

CRABTREE
PUBLISHING COMPANY
WWW.CRABTREEBOOKS.COM

CRABTREE
PUBLISHING COMPANY
WWW.CRABTREEBOOKS.COM

Author: Linda Barghoorn

Editors: Sarah Eason, Harriet McGregor, Wendy Scavuzzo, and Janine Deschenes

Proofreader and indexer: Wendy Scavuzzo

Editorial director: Kathy Middleton

Design: Paul Myerscough and Jessica Moon

Cover design: Paul Myerscough and Jessica Moon

Photo research: Rachel Blount

Production coordinator and Prepress technician: Ken Wright

Print coordinator: Katherine Berti

Consultants: Hawa Sabriye and HaEun Kim, Centre for Refugee Studies, York University

Produced for Crabtree Publishing Company by Calcium Creative

Publisher's Note: The story presented in this book is a fictional account based on extensive research of real-life accounts by refugees, with the aim of reflecting the true experience of refugee children and their families.

Photo Credits:
t=Top, bl=Bottom Left, br=Bottom Right

Inside: Jessica Moon: pp. 16t, 29b; Shutterstock: AlexAranda: p. 17l; Atlaspix: p. 6t; Best-Backgrounds: pp. 22-23; Hugo Brizard – YouGoPhoto: p. 7t; Brothers Good: p. 6b; Kobby Dagan: pp. 12c, 12b, 13; Stefano Ember: pp. 5, 8c, 8b; FedBul: pp. 20-21b; Fotos593: p. 17r; Guayo Fuentes: p. 4; ES James: p. 10l; Loca4motion: p. 9t; Ian MacLellan: pp. 14, 16c, 18-19t; Macrovector: pp. 3, 15t; Milosz Maslanka: p. 20; MSSA: pp. 28, 29tl; Chess Ocampo: p. 18b; Panda Vector: pp. 10t, 26t; PlatypusMi86: p. 9b; Matyas Rehak: p. 11; Rvector: p. 21t; Rinat Sultanov: p. 7b; Syda Productions: pp. 14-15b; Jne Valokuvaus: p. 25bl; © UNHCR: © UNHCR/Tito Herrera: p. 29tr; © UNHCR/Laura Padoan: pp. 23, 24-25t; © UNHCR/Encarni Pindado: p. 27; © UNHCR/Markel Redondo: pp. 22, 26bl, 26br; © UNHCR/Daniele Volpe: pp. 21bl, 21br, 25r.

Cover: Jessica Moon; Shutterstock: Nadzeya Shanchuk.

Library and Archives Canada Cataloguing in Publication

Barghoorn, Linda, author
    A refugee's journey from El Salvador / Linda Barghoorn.

(Leaving my homeland)
Includes index.
Issued in print and electronic formats.
ISBN 978-0-7787-4685-0 (hardcover).--
ISBN 978-0-7787-4691-1 (softcover).--
ISBN 978-1-4271-2069-4 (HTML)

    1. Refugees--El Salvador--Juvenile literature. 2. Refugees--Mexico--Juvenile literature. 3. Refugee children--El Salvador--Juvenile literature. 4. Refugee children--Mexico--Juvenile literature. 5. Refugees--Social conditions--Juvenile literature. 6. El Salvador--Social conditions--Juvenile literature. I. Title.

HV640.5.S24B36 2018   j305.9'06914097284   C2017-907644-2
                                                          C2017-907645-0

Library of Congress Cataloging-in-Publication Data

Names: Barghoorn, Linda, author.
Title: A refugee's journey from El Salvador / Linda Barghoorn.
Description: New York : Crabtree Publishing, [2018] |
    Series: Leaving my homeland | Includes index.
Identifiers: LCCN 2017054806 (print) | LCCN 2017057139 (ebook) |
    ISBN 9781427120694 (Electronic HTML) |
    ISBN 9780778746850 (reinforced library binding : alk. paper) |
    ISBN 9780778746911 (pbk. : alk. paper)
Subjects: LCSH: Refugee children--El Salvador--Juvenile literature. |
    Refugees--El Salvador--Juvenile literature. | El Salvador--Emigration
    and immigration--Juvenile literature.
Classification: LCC HV640.5.C46 (ebook) | LCC HV640.5.C46 B37 2018
    (print) | DDC 305.9/06914097284--dc23
LC record available at https://lccn.loc.gov/2017054806

Crabtree Publishing Company
www.crabtreebooks.com   1-800-387-7650

Printed in the U.S.A./022018/CG20171220

Published in Canada
Crabtree Publishing
616 Welland Ave.
St. Catharines, Ontario
L2M 5V6

Published in the United States
Crabtree Publishing
PMB 59051
350 Fifth Avenue, 59th Floor
New York, New York 10118

Published in the United Kingdom
Crabtree Publishing
Maritime House
Basin Road North, Hove
BN41 1WR

Published in Australia
Crabtree Publishing
3 Charles Street
Coburg North
VIC, 3058

What Is in This Book?

Leaving El Salvador

Many people in El Salvador suffer from **poverty** and lack of jobs. Half of the country's population lives in the countryside. Their homes have no electricity or running water. In the capital city of San Salvador, wealthy people live in clean, modern houses.

In 1980, the **inequality** between the wealthy and the poor caused a **civil war**. It lasted until 1992. Thousands fled to escape the violence. Many Salvadorans, or people from El Salvador, fled to the United States. Others joined gangs. Gangs are organized groups of criminals. They spread violence and take part in **illegal** activities.

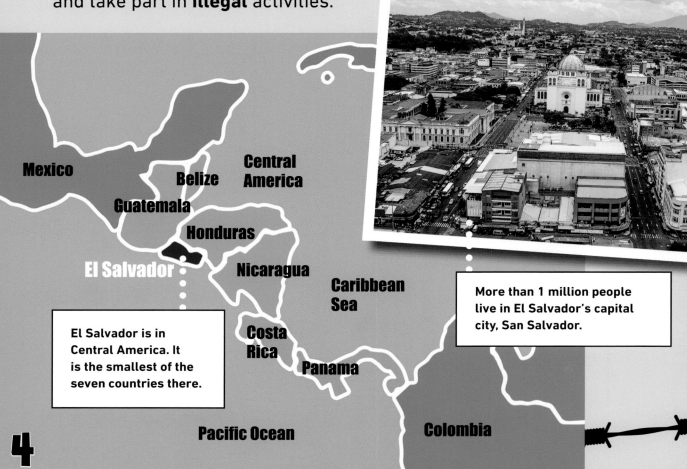

Mexico

Central America

Belize

Guatemala

Honduras

El Salvador

Nicaragua

Caribbean Sea

Costa Rica

Panama

Pacific Ocean

Colombia

More than 1 million people live in El Salvador's capital city, San Salvador.

El Salvador is in Central America. It is the smallest of the seven countries there.

Every child has rights. Rights are privileges and freedoms that are protected by law. **Refugees** have the right to special protection and help. The **United Nations (UN)** Convention on the Rights of the Child is a document that lists the rights of children all over the world. Think about these rights as you read this book.

El Salvador has a population of more than 6.5 million people. There are few jobs available in the country. These men make a living by fishing for lobster.

After the war ended, those who had fled were excited to return home. But the country soon faced new problems. Gang violence in El Salvador did not go away. Crime, violence, and killings continued even after the war. As the police tried to remove the gangs, the violence grew worse. Many innocent people were killed.

Thousands fled their homes to escape. Some live as **internally displaced persons (IDPs)**. IDPs are people who have been forced to live somewhere else in their country. Many more became refugees. Refugees are people who flee their **homeland** because of war and other unsafe conditions. Refugees are different from **immigrants**. Immigrants choose to leave to look for better opportunities in another country.

My Homeland, El Salvador

El Salvador is the smallest country in Central America. It shares borders with Guatemala and Honduras. El Salvador is sometimes known as the Land of Volcanoes, because of the many volcanoes found there. Rain forests once covered much of the land. But the rain forests were cleared to create space for growing coffee. There are now few trees to slow the flow of water. So, the country often suffers from mudslides and floods.

The blue stripes of El Salvador's flag represent the two oceans that surround Central America. The white stripe represents peace.

A long line of volcanoes runs through the center of El Salvador.

San Salvador

The population of El Salvador is made up of Spanish and **Indigenous** peoples. Hundreds of years ago, the Pipil people were the main tribe in the region. Their territory is named *Cuscatlán*, which means "Land of the Jewel." Spanish people first arrived in El Salvador and took control in the 1500s. They controlled the country until 1821, when it became **independent**.

Many people in El Salvador are farmers. Important crops include cocoa, coffee, sugar, corn, and rice. Some farmers also raise cattle. Today, typical meals often include rice, beans, and tortillas, which are a type of flatbread. Most people cannot afford to eat meat. Many Salvadorans do not have enough food to eat every day. **Malnutrition** is one of the leading causes of death among the country's poor people.

Dramatic volcanoes dominate El Salvador's central region.

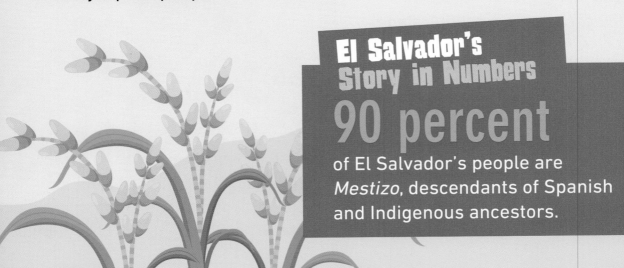

El Salvador's Story in Numbers

90 percent

of El Salvador's people are *Mestizo*, descendants of Spanish and Indigenous ancestors.

Benito's Story: My Life in El Salvador

I grew up in a village outside San Salvador. My parents ran a small grocery store in the neighborhood near our home. My grandparents, aunties, and uncles lived close by with their families. My parents worked long days at the store. So, our families shared preparing meals and taking care of the children. Our families were very close and always celebrated birthdays and holidays together.

We lived in a small house. It was often filled with the delicious smells of my grandmother's cooking. I have two brothers and two sisters, so our home was crowded and noisy. Every day after school, I met my friends to play soccer in the field nearby. Like most kids in El Salvador, we were crazy about soccer.

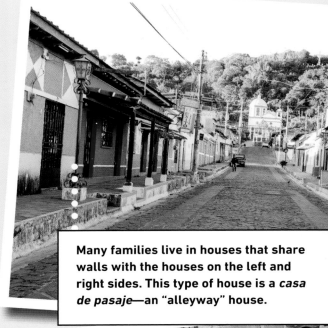

Many families live in houses that share walls with the houses on the left and right sides. This type of house is a *casa de pasaje*—an "alleyway" house.

Soccer is a favorite pastime in El Salvador.

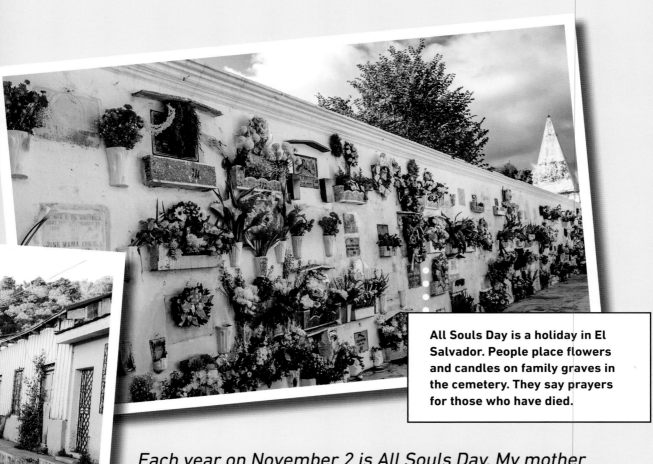

All Souls Day is a holiday in El Salvador. People place flowers and candles on family graves in the cemetery. They say prayers for those who have died.

Each year on November 2 is All Souls Day. My mother cooked a meal of tortillas, corn, beans, and rice. After lunch, our family visited the cemetery. We honored our family members who had died. Later in the day, everyone gathered in the village square. We celebrated late into the night with music. My family loved to laugh, sing, and spend time together.

UN Rights of the Child

You have the right to live with a family who cares for you.

The Conflict in El Salvador

Violence between police and gangs has caused thousands of deaths.

El Salvador has struggled with problems of poverty. There is little access to land for the poor. Farmers and Indigenous people began to protest for help from the government. But they were arrested, kidnapped, or killed. **Rebel groups** promised the poor better rights. They began a civil war with the government in 1980. Many people fled the country.

El Salvador's Story in Numbers

The government of El Salvador claims that nearly

500,000

people are connected to the gangs. They are either family members or people cooperating with the gangs.

The UN created a peace agreement in 1992. El Salvador hoped for a better future. Many Salvadorans were happy to return home. But thousands who had lived illegally in the United States were deported, or forced to leave the country. They returned to El Salvador. But they were again faced with poverty and a lack of jobs and education. They were forced back into gang activity so they could make money to survive.

Ordinary people were often caught in the middle of gang violence.

Enemy gangs fought for power and money. The police used violence to try to get rid of the gangs. When the gangs fought back, many were killed on both sides.

Gangs forced families to pay them for protection from the police and other gangs. When poor families could not afford to pay them, the gangs threatened them. As the violence grew worse, many fled the country.

Benito's Story: The Gangs Move In

I was 11 years old when the trouble began. The gangs had arrived in our village. Members of one gang began to visit my parents' store. They demanded money. At first, my mother tried to make them happy by giving them some food. But they soon insisted that my parents pay them. They wanted money in exchange for protection against other gangs.

Many women in El Salvador work to help support their families.

Ordinary people and businesses in El Salvador's villages were forced to pay money to the gangs.

Some of the gang members were students. They came to our store every day after school. Their threats became louder and angrier. My older brother Juan recognized some of the boys from his class. He wanted to report them. My parents were afraid to call the police. They worried that this would make the gang angrier. That would put us all in more danger.

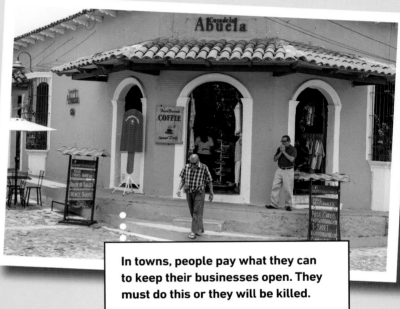

In towns, people pay what they can to keep their businesses open. They must do this or they will be killed.

My parents had to keep the store open. They needed to earn money to pay for our family's food, clothing, and school supplies. So, they paid the gangs money every month and tried to protect us.

The gangs threatened other families in our village. Some of my brother's friends were forced to join them. When one tried to escape, he disappeared. My 14-year-old sister Gabriela received threats from classmates at school. Usually, they wanted her to help them cheat on a test. "If you do not help, you will be in trouble," they warned. Then one day, Juan disappeared on his way home from school.

Why People Flee

So many people have been killed in El Salvador that the country has become known as the most dangerous place on Earth outside a war zone. Violence is part of everyday life in El Salvador. Children do not know what it is like to grow up in a peaceful, safe environment.

Families live in fear of losing their children to gangs and violence. Gangs force teenage boys and girls to become members. If they refuse, they are beaten or killed. Children in the gangs often experience **abuse** and violence from other gang members. Gangs force members to take part in criminal activities.

Salvadoran parents fear for their children's safety.

El Salvador's Story in Numbers

There are about

50,000

gang members in El Salvador. Some are as young as nine years old.

Cities in El Salvador are divided between the gangs. Different gangs control different areas.

As the gangs have gained power, there are few people to turn to for help. Teachers at school are frightened by student gang members. Police are afraid to enter communities to protect people. Even churches have been threatened. Families who try to hide their children from the gangs are threatened if they do not hand them over.

Nowhere is safe in El Salvador. Parents who are desperate to save their children have fled the country with their families. Some families are too poor to leave together. They send their children away alone and hope they reach safety in another country. Many Salvadorans must make a choice. They can face violence and death at home. Or they can make an illegal and dangerous journey to freedom in a new country.

Benito's Story: Decision Time

My parents searched everywhere for Juan. Finally, they went to the police. The police refused to help. There was no sign of Juan. It was as if he had vanished from Earth. My brothers, sisters, and I cried and cried. We were afraid for Juan. What if he never came home?

Then one of the gang members threatened to take me and my sister Gabriela. My parents took us out of school. They hoped the gang would forget about us. But they soon came to our home, demanding that we come outside. They shouted threats through the door. My mother held her breath.

Some families kept children home from school to try to keep them safe. But they were often not safe there, either.

Occasionally, if I went outside, I would see the gang members. One day, one of the boys called out to me as I hurried by. "You will join your brother soon if you and your sister do not agree to come to us." I ran home in fear to tell my parents what they had said. My parents were terrified. It was becoming impossible for them to protect us.

El Salvador's Story in Numbers
1 in 10
Salvadoran children is forced to leave school to avoid gang violence and bullying.

Benito's parents searched the nearby villages for Juan.

In some gangs, members use hand signs to identify one another.

Two weeks later, the gang returned to my parents' store. They said, "You will give us Gabriela and Benito by tomorrow or bad things will happen to your family." When my father argued with them, they beat him. We were all in shock. My mother said we must leave.

17

On the Run

Salvadorans who leave their homeland face difficult choices about where to go. The neighboring countries of Guatemala, Nicaragua, and Honduras also have problems with violence and gangs. Some people travel to Costa Rica. They have friends or family there who can help support them. Most refugees from El Salvador hope to reach the United States through Mexico. But the risks are high. Many are sent back to their homeland when they are caught crossing the US border illegally.

Thousands of children have been forced to flee without their families.

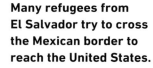

Many refugees from El Salvador try to cross the Mexican border to reach the United States.

UN Rights of the Child

You have the right to an identity, which no one can take away from you.

Some refugees seek **asylum** in Mexico because they are afraid of getting caught crossing the US border. The **United Nations High Commissioner for Refugees (UNHCR)** provides some money. This helps refugees pay for housing and food as they begin new lives there.

Much of the **foreign aid** given to El Salvador does not support the refugees. Instead, organizations such as Cáritas and Save the Children try to help support and rebuild safe communities in the country. They want to provide a better future for El Salvador's youth so fewer people will be forced to flee.

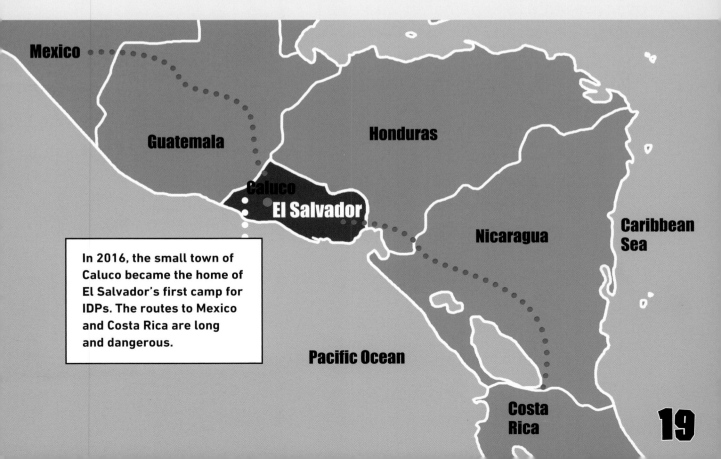

In 2016, the small town of Caluco became the home of El Salvador's first camp for IDPs. The routes to Mexico and Costa Rica are long and dangerous.

Mexico

Guatemala

Honduras

Caluco

El Salvador

Nicaragua

Caribbean Sea

Pacific Ocean

Costa Rica

19

Benito's Story: Running for Our Lives

That night, we each packed a small bag of clothes. We said goodbye to our family. There was no time to say goodbye to friends. Mother did not want anyone else to know we were leaving. She was afraid the gang would stop us if they found out.

Mother asked my auntie to take over our store. She gathered whatever money we had, and borrowed some from our relatives. The next morning, while it was still dark, we walked to the bus station. We boarded a bus to take us through Guatemala to the border at Mexico. It was late that evening when we arrived near the border. We spent the night curled up on the hard ground. We were cold, hungry, and scared.

The bus journey to Mexico takes around 12 hours.

*The next morning, Mother found a **trafficker**, known as a coyote, to help us cross into Mexico. After she had paid him, there was little money left. We waited until dark to set off on foot. When my younger brother and sister got tired, Mother, Gabriela, and I took turns carrying them. Finally, we reached a river. The trafficker pointed to Mexico on the other side.*

He took us to a small, wobbly boat. He paddled us across the river. We were shivering in fear. My mother and sisters did not know how to swim. They were afraid of drowning. Finally, we reached the other side. The strange man left us without a word.

Refugees cross the border into Mexico by taking a boat across the Suchiate River. This helps them enter the country without being stopped, but it is also dangerous. Many people drown.

These people are trying to cross the Suchiate River in a raft made of rubber tires and wooden planks.

Where Do Refugees Go?

Canada: 1,230

United States: 14,332

Mexico: 2,366

Three out of four people fleeing El Salvador want to go the United States. Some have family or friends there who can help and support them. But the journey has many risks. There may be long walks and dangerous river crossings. There are criminals and tightly guarded borders. Many refugees have been killed or hurt, or have died along the way.

This map shows where the Salvadoran refugees went.

Refugees often suffer **exploitation** and abuse. Gangs often target refugees. They may kidnap children. They then demand a **ransom** from their families before setting them free.

Traffickers often take advantage of refugees. They leave them stranded in **isolated** places. Refugees must continue the journey on their own.

In 2016, **19,595** refugees fled El Salvador. Most traveled to the United States, Mexico, and Canada. Some traveled to Costa Rica, Panama, and Belize.

These children are exhausted after traveling to Mexico from El Salvador.

Refugees who cross borders illegally might be sent to prison. They are then sent back home to face the gangs again. In 2017, President Trump announced he planned to build a wall on the Mexican border. He wants to stop illegal immigration into the United States. This would mean that Salvadoran refugees would have more difficulty finding safety.

Benito's Story: Starting Over

We walked and walked until we reached a road. The Mexican police found us. They took us to a building where other refugees were also held. Mother and Father filled out paperwork and whispered to the other people. They hoped to find out what might happen next. Finally, a local aid agency took us to a shelter. There, we could apply for asylum.

Two months later, we learned our application was successful. We felt so lucky. We had watched many children and families be sent back to the dangers of El Salvador.

We have moved into a tiny house. It has mattresses for beds, a few pots and pans, and a dresser for our clothes. We are all back in school now. I am happy to be there, but I have missed a lot of work. Mother and Father get a little money each month to help pay for groceries and rent. Mother also cleans houses and takes care of neighborhood children. She earns money for school supplies and clothes. Father is looking for work.

Refugee children miss a lot of school. It can be hard to catch up when they are back in school.

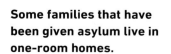

Some families that have been given asylum live in one-room homes.

24

It is scary starting our lives over without Juan. But at least we are safe. It is lonely though. We miss our family and friends. We sometimes hear news from back home. The gangs have threatened my auntie who runs our store. She thinks she will also have to leave soon. No one has heard from Juan. We pray that he is alive and will find us. I hope we can someday return home to a safe and happy life in El Salvador.

Life in a new school in a new country is challenging.

Challenges Refugees Face

For the refugees who arrive safely in a new country, there are still many challenges. Often, they receive little help to complete their asylum claims. They also face uncertainty about whether their claim will be accepted. Many are rejected. Some governments believe they can be returned home to a different area where they will be safe. But the truth is that there are few safe places in El Salvador these days.

Salvadoran refugees in Mexico do whatever work they can find. These men are selling flowers.

Some refugees enter training programs to learn skills that will help them find jobs.

UN Rights of the Child

You have the right to protection
from any kind of exploitation.

Refugees who can claim asylum in
other countries often face poverty
and **discrimination**. They may need
help from aid organizations to begin
a new life. Often, refugees are lonely,
isolated, and homesick.

Refugees are also vulnerable as
they try to begin new lives in a
new country. They often lack the
education, skills, or opportunities
to get jobs. They may need to go back
to school to learn English and gain
new skills. Many Salvadorans cannot
afford medicine and health care.
Without good jobs, many refugees
have no choice but to enter back into
gang activity. They need to support
themselves and their families. This
repeats the violence that refugees
escaped from.

**Many Salvadorans face
discrimination from the local
communities. Local people worry
that they may bring violence
with them from their homeland.**

You Can Help!

There are many things you can do to help newcomers and refugees in your community. These are just a few ideas.

☑ Speak out against discrimination when you see it happening.

☑ Welcome a newcomer in your community. Offer to help them with their English or learn a few words of their language.

☑ Participate in fundraising activities such as clothing or food drives. This supports refugees in your community.

☑ Take part in World Refugee Day on June 20 every year.

☑ Share with your friends and family what you have learned about refugees in this book.

☑ Invite a newcomer to your home for a meal, or accept an invitation to their home.

El Salvador's Story in Numbers

It is estimated that

2 million

people of Salvadoran origin live in the United States.

Young people in El Salvador want to live a life without fear of the gangs.

Discussion Prompts

1. Why are so many people from El Salvador fleeing their country?

2. How would you feel if you had to leave your family, home, and country to stay alive?

3. Explain the difference between a refugee, an immigrant, and an IDP.

Glossary

abuse Being harmed or hurt by someone

asylum Protection given to refugees by a country

civil war A war between groups of people in the same country

discrimination The unfair treatment of someone based on gender, race, religion, or other identifiers

exploitation Taking unfair advantage of someone

foreign aid Assistance given by organizations or governments from outside the country

homeland The country where someone was born or grew up

illegal Against the law

immigrants People who leave one country to live in another

independent Free from outside control

Indigenous Referring to people who have lived in a region for a long time, or are native to it

inequality An unfair situation in which some people have more rights than others

internally displaced persons (IDPs) People who are forced from their homes during a conflict, but remain in their country

isolated Far from people or cut off from people

malnutrition Sickness caused by not having enough healthy food

poverty The state of being very poor and having few belongings

ransom Money that is demanded or paid to free a kidnapped person

rebel groups People who fight against the government of a country

refugees People who flee from their own country to another due to unsafe conditions

trafficker A person who illegally moves people or drugs for money

United Nations (UN) An international organization that promotes peace between countries and helps refugees

United Nations High Commissioner for Refugees (UNHCR) A program that protects and supports refugees everywhere

Learning More

Books

Argueta, Jorge. *We Are Like the Clouds*. Groundwood Books, 2016.

Markovics, Joyce. *El Salvador* (Countries We Come From). Bearport Publishing, 2016.

Simmons, Walter. *El Salvador* (Exploring Countries). Bellwether Media, 2012.

Websites

http://easyscienceforkids.com/all-about-el-salvador
Discover facts about El Salvador, including a 10-minute video slideshow about El Salvador's geography, landscapes, and people.

http://mrnussbaum.com/el-salvador-for-kids
Visit this website for pictures, descriptions, and some interesting facts about El Salvador's important cities and geographic sites.

www.unicef.org/rightsite/files/uncrcchilldfriendlylanguage.pdf
Learn more about the United Nations Convention on the Rights of the Child.

Index

About the Author

Linda Barghoorn studied languages in university because she wanted to travel the world. She has visited 56 countries, taking photographs and learning about different people and cultures. Her father traveled to North America as a German immigrant more than 50 years ago. Linda has written 14 children's books and is writing a novel about her father's life.